Inspire U

"Where the School of Thought is positivity"

3/31/2011

Dr. Salima K. N'Dulu
©

INSPIRE U
ORIGINAL 2010
REVISED 4/2012

LIBRARY OF CONGRESS CATALOGING-
IN-PUBLICATION DATA
NDulu, Salima Kim, 1966-
Inspire U/Salima K. NDulu, PhD
TXu001701463 / 2010-06-28
ISBN 978-0-615-62632-1

Contents

Introduction..i

Foreword...iii

Chapter One: **Get Used To Feeling Better**..........1

Chapter Two: **Art Imitating Life**........................6

Chapter Three: **Taking Up Basket Weaving**......15

Chapter Four: **Guilt**.......................................19

Chapter Five: **Spiritual ADHD**......................26

Chapter Six: **Dark times Light**.......................31

Chapter Seven: **Build, Build & Rebuild**............37

Chapter Eight: **Future Shock**.........................45

Chapter Nine: **What in the World**..................50

Chapter Ten: **Life's 'What ifs'**.......................55

Chapter Eleven: **A Look At Relationships**........59

Charter Twelve: **Respect, Nothing More**..........66

Chapter Thirteen: **Life's Miracles**...................71

Chapter Fourteen: **Taking Back**.....................76

Chapter Fifteen: **From Caterpillars**.................81

Chapter Sixteen: **The Power to Create**............85

Chapter Seventeen: **Sometimes Expectation**.......92

Chapter Eighteen: **God's Hands**....................99

Introduction

Writing this book was definitely a labor of love for me and to you. I remember needing inspiration at my lowest points and appreciating it at my highest points. "Inspire U" is meant to do just as the title states; it's filled with little bits of wisdom that I've learned over the years. This book has surprised me, but then again we are all created from Greatness to be great. These words didn't actually come 'from' me; I would say they came 'through' me. So, many times I would be so inspired by a person, place or thing that I had to write about it. There have been many books that have been written to motivate and inspire. These books help others to see their own greatness; my wish is for this book to work hand in hand with those books.

As you go on your literary journey inside this book, I hope you feel so inspired that your spirits are lifted and that you feel that you have gained some wisdom. To seek spiritual knowledge is the wisest of actions-it feeds the mind and the spirit. Once you discover your truths for yourself, you are less likely to be swayed in another direction, because your truth is the center of your being. Your truth dictates how you think, how you feel and how you act. If you are dedicated and committed to 'your' truth, you will have a fuller and richer spiritual life, in fact, you will evolve in ways you never thought possible.

Thank you for allowing my words to become a part of your spiritual journey and that you enjoy the process.

Many Blessings & Good Times;

Dr. Salima NDulu

Foreword

I am grateful to be here and to share the inspiration that has come through me and not from me. I have evolved as a spiritual person from childhood into adulthood, learning who I thought God was then and who I feel God is to me now. I was Divinely inspired to write "Inspire U" a long time ago. There have been many nights where I have been in a sound sleep and was awaken suddenly with an idea or story to write. This book followed many years of ministerial and spiritual studying. I began my spiritual studies in the traditional churches, the Episcopal Church was my home and I love to visit from time to time. During my time as an Episcopalian, I also attended Catholic Schools.

This began my open minded approach to religion in general. Learning that other people believed in something different than what I believed gave me a desire to learn more. My mother was a supervisor of a Jewish newspaper, another religion that was very different from mine, fueled another desire to learn more. Once I experienced a variety of religions and spiritualities, I decided to eventually become formally educated in Religious Studies. The Society of Novus Spiritus assisted me in the first leg of my journey. I started taking ministerial classes through the Alliance of Divine Love, that was an amazing set of courses and once I had taken several other courses in religion and spiritual studies, The Esoteric Theological Seminary provided me with another avenue to become licensed and degreed in Pastoral Counseling and Religious Studies. The idea of providing inspiration and assistance to people who wish to learn about different types of spirituality is very rewarding. What I have discovered in my studies is that most religions have more similarities than they have differences. It's the similarities that should bring us together and the differences that we should accept and not let them separate us. When it's all said and done, the end result is Love. We are supposed to love one another and it feels much better to spread love than to lend energy to its opposite and negative counterpart. The title of this book speaks for itself; it is here to inspire each and every one of you. Relax, Enjoy and Be Inspired.

Acknowledgments

I'd first like to thank God for being my main inspiration, my divine source and for giving me the words to put on paper. I thank my ancestors, especially late Grandparents: Rev. Henry Williams, Elizabeth Williams and David McCauley, for it is on their shoulders, in which I stand to achieve greatness. I definitely thank my Mother, Sylvia Smith, who has been there every step of the way and has passed down her gift of writing. I would like to thank my Fathers, William Rollins, Richard Sowell, Wilbert Tolliver & Elder A. James Smith, each one of you have added your own joy to my life. I have the best mentors. To all of my parents, I love you more than I can say.

I want to thank my soul-mate, Mark Young, I cherish our years together and look forward to many more. To my children, the ones I've raised and the new ones: Clarence, Deidre, Alaina, Dewayne, Tarik, Aubrey, Roumell, Marik, Yamisha and my grandchildren, Jayde and Jaiden for being the best of the best. Stand on my shoulders and look to the Heavens and know that *God is the only thing greater than you*. I love you…

To all of my family, I love each and every one of you. To my Aunt Victoria who has double duty as my editor as well, thank you for helping my words make sense. As for the rest of my family, there are too many to possibly name individually, but I have to name my Grandma Mary, Grandma Evelyn, Aunt Diana, Uncle James, Uncle Ronald, Uncle Edward, Uncle Tony, Missy, Angela, LaTisha, Dawn, Destiny, Marcus, Robert Jr, Robert III, Jaheim, Sherrie, Ronell, Sean, Brian, Saladin, Barbara, Erica, James Jr, Courtney, Denaea, April, Chris, Mark, Tim, Robert W., Beth, Moses, Emmanuel, Sela, Noah, Juanita,

Andre (Moe) and the rest I could not name all of you- running out of paper. (SMILE). Most of you are so far away and I miss you terribly. I hope to have that reunion sooner than later. I love you.

To the *Unity Church of Fort Lauderdale*, Both of the *Unity Churches of Jacksonville* & *Unity On the Bay* in Florida, thank you for being my church homes and for feeding my spirit. I'd like to thank all of the spiritual teachers that have written books to inspire as I'd hope to do. I'd like to thank Angel, who pushed me to finish this book and Mary P., who kept me sane during the end of this project. Thanks to K. Roland Williams, a great writer and friend.

"Life is full of experiences; these experiences help us to grow and to evolve."

Inspire U
The Beginning

CHAPTER ONE

Get Used To Feeling Better.

"Today I will give up one bad habit and trade it for a new good one".

Get Used To Feeling Better.

Most of us get used to many things. We get used to jobs, relationships, friends, family or whatever. We get used to being fat, skinny, tall or short. We change hairstyles, old clothes, buy new things, but we sometimes just get used to feeling bad.

It's funny; we never give a second thought to feeling great. In our smiling all of the time or knowing that we *can* feel good, we will learn that when it rains in life, the sunshine isn't far behind. We look at everything in our lives mainly as a challenge and that can be tiring, but if we look at those same situations through optimistic eyes, everything changes its appearance. Just like, the magician or illusionist can make you see what they want you to see. "Beauty is in the eye of the beholder". This means that one person's view or opinion is their perception of their reality.

Let's direct this to you, now you make a life that is so puzzling that it seems impossible for

you to be happy or successful. What 'road blocks' are you putting up for yourself? What is the reason for your lack? Lack of accomplishment? Lack of money? Lack of Love? Lack! Lack! Lack! What do you plan to do with your life or what do you plan to do with your lack? Life is more than working everyday; day after day and coming home doing what your routine calls for you to do.
YOU DESERVE SO MUCH MORE THAN THAT!

Let's break it down. You say, "I want happiness, success, you know-the good life."

Well, what will it take to achieve that 'good life' that you desire? I'll tell you. Good Living starts with Good Thinking (continuous good thinking).

Why don't we venture back to the things we are used to? Habits we need to obtain and ones not worthy of our time and effort. We get used to not having situations work in our favor, so we just bow down to defeat. We get used to being 'financially challenged' until payday rolls around again. The idea of not having money is not the major issue-the problem is how we got that way in the first place and how we see our situation. If you say that you're '*broke*', it implies that there is something wrong with you. If you turn the same situation around and speak of not having money at this moment only-remaining optimistic, then you open the doors for wealth to enter at a later date. This gives a positive spin on a temporary issue. Now not having money right now is just an example, if we take this route to dealing with other situations in life, we will have success in ways we never knew existed. As we begin to turn negative situations into positive words, thoughts and deeds, we will begin gaining and creating the habit of 'feeling better'.

<u>WHAT MAKES ME FEEL BETTER?</u>

CHANGE YOUR MIND

It's about time to walk inside the mind,
the mind that houses thoughts,
the thoughts that create things,
the things that cause life to happen.

Watch the direction of your mind, because
your thoughts blindly follow it creating the things
that you may not want to happen,
yet you have the nerve to be
unhappy with your life, why? You created it-
right?

Think thoughts that are good in nature.
Measure the depths of you mind so,
shallow thoughts will drown in the deepness of
you.
Change negative thinking, for they are so far
away from the mind of GOD
Change it up so your life won't stray from good
Change it, it will make you smile.
Change it-just because.
Change your mindset and your life will follow.

CHAPTER TWO
Art Imitating Life

"Life is how you see it, what you make it and where you take it."

Art Imitating Life

"You are the artist who holds the brush to paint the life you lead or want to lead. You hold the colors that brighten or darken your life. As children, we have this wide-eyed optimism of what we want for our grown up lives. No matter how bad the childhood may have been, there were dreams of a better grown-up life.

I wanted a red Corvette and a big house with lots of stuff, now I had no idea what it took to achieve these things, but the dream was still there. Sometimes when we paint our lives, we may miss a stroke or dip our brush into the wrong color, but as long as we keep on dipping and stroking we are still in the game.

Obstacles are meant to strengthen and teach us lessons-so pick up that brush and paint a big mountain in your path. Paint yourself climbing it, because if you don't paint it, someone else will-Meaning, if you don't prepare for those tough times, you will fall hard. Preparation for what is to come, is not the same as being pessimistic, thus causing something bad to occur due to our negative energy flow. Preparation is actually life's "Plan B or C". You prepare for financial hardship by saving money in the bank. You prepare for a hurricane or snowstorm by purchasing needed supplies like food, water, medicine and the like. Paint these things in your life's picture, the trial, the survival and potential outcome.

Life is like a box, you are constantly putting things into it and removing the non-essentials from it (people also fall into this category). We, as thinking individuals have the ability to figure our way in and out of various situations- using our *paintbrushes*.

Many times our mind and out paintbrushes are not on the same page, just like when we enter into relationships, we have reality versus what we really want to see.
Our paintbrush is painting blue skies and our minds are signally '*red flags*!' Our paintbrushes

must be on one accord with reality or else we will paint ourselves into a great big mess. Ask yourselves, "What is it that I want from life?" "What is life willing to give me?" "What steps do I take or what am I willing to do or give up in order to have the life that I so desire?" It's all about the thought or the desire. Then you have to pick up brush, your assorted colors of paint must be opened and ready, now you are ready to paint this picture we call life.

People say things like "Today is the first day of the rest of your life." I would phrase it like this: "This is the first brushstroke to paint the picture, of the rest of your life." We all have a beautiful picture inside of us, sometimes it looks bleak and colorless, but the good news is that we can pick any color-mix any color in order to brighten our future. Life is ever-changing, so our picture will never be the same, it changes with us. Our pictures never look like anyone else's-the similarities are just that, but all of our lives (pictures) are unique and beautiful in their own way.

Today I may feel like painting yellow, yesterday I was in a red mood, who knows what colors tomorrow will bring out. There is no fear needed here, only for you to be completely honest with yourself as you paint.
If you paint lies, your mind will notice and your picture will be out of sync with you and the universe. One thing about the paintbrush of the soul and the mind-they would rather work together for success, than to be on opposing sides creating failure. Failure is one of those mountains in your path, but some failures could be avoided by nice even strokes and the union of the mind and soul (i.e. the paintbrush and reality).

Painting life can be pleasant one minute and it can be unpleasant the next, so just go with it and never give up. Never get angry and toss your paintbrush into the air, you never know where the paint might land. It could land right on top of your head-now you have red and blue paint dripping all over your face-not a pretty sight. Now what? You have dots of uncertainty splattered on your picture and it's a mess that you now must clean up before you can start painting again. You can clean it or you can even paint the whole thing white and start your picture all over again. That's the beauty of life, you can start over and do things differently and have a whole new perspective on life because you are older and hopefully wiser. As long as you are still breathing, you can paint new pictures into your life. Remember life is like a picture, it has many colors, many sides and directions. It changes every second, so just flow along with it and continue to paint until your heart's content. Skies of Blue, Clouds so White, The Greenest Grass and Brightest Yellow Sunlight. Keep your paintbrush in tune with reality and paint! PAINT YOUR LIFE. PAINT YOUR LIFE! PAINT IT BEAUTIFUL!! COLORFUL!!!

WHAT KIND OF LIFE AM I CREATING?

THE RAIN

The rain falls on the flowers and the trees,
so that they can grow and create beauty.
The rain falls in your life so that you can grow
mentally and spiritually allowing you to create
and express your own degree of beauty.
That beauty that radiates from you can also add
sunshine to someone else's rainy day.

CHAPTER THREE

Take Up Basket Weaving

"Bring to yourself the best of everything and that *you* will never be disappointed."

Salima N'Dulu

Take Up Basket Weaving

Boredom is often the source of many of the problems in our lives. When children become bored, they get often into trouble, it's not any different with adults; we just find alternate means of trouble to get into. To be alone on a Saturday night or dateless on the weekends tends to cause many of us to become sad, lonely and depressed. Sadness creates many negative thought and actions. We may place ourselves in situations that we don't need to be in, by either going to places that we do not need to be or spending time with individuals that do not bring out the best in us. I remember telling my elder relatives that I was bored, but that was usually followed by an invitation to assist with housework, being told to read a book or one of the more sarcastic members of the family would reply "Take up basket weaving." Sarcasm is wasted on those who don't understand, because there was nothing more boring to a ten year old than the thought of weaving a basket.

There is another saying, "An idle mind is the devil's workshop." Nothing rings more true, because once we become idle, the mind may not take us to our proper way of thinking all because of boredom. There are so many constructive things we could be doing, but boredom becomes an excuse for doing many of those things that cause us trouble. Our inner child wins the battle of the wills.

Although the thought of sitting still and weaving anything, sounds less than exciting, let's figure what are those things that would give you the fulfillment that you deserve. In a country that is a melting pot of culture, learning about other cultures requires research and in the long run is definitely not boring, it's actually very exciting. Once that culture is explored, learning about the customs and the foods, the learning the language should come next, now that is something to really keep you occupied. This is just one example of avoiding boredom and basket weaving, so to speak.

Improving your life comes one step at a time. Think of some of the things that you have always wanted to do in the past. This is a good time to start planning to do one or two of them now. Go on that cruise, take that class, learn to speak Mandarin Chinese or Spanish, how about ballet or salsa lessons or anything else that runs through your mind. Instead of feeling like you missed something in life, you will have a lot more fun being productive for yourself. The truth is, basket weaving is a beautiful form of self expression and yields beautiful results, who knows what your basket will say about you. Live as if this is your last day on earth, enjoy every minute and allow yourself time to be you.

WHAT BRINGS ME EXCITEMENT?

CHAPTER FOUR
Guilt

"Guilt is useless, guilt's no fun, guilt's no good for anyone. If you live inside of guilt, how can you see the light".

__Guilt__

There is no place for guilt in the spiritually enlightened mind or for any mind for that matter. Life can calculate a number of things that one could feel guilty about, but the mind should work to subtract them from our consciousness. There are loads of guilt being heaped upon our shoulders becoming heavier and heavier, sometimes too heavy for our small bodies to carry. Life was not meant to be saddled with guilt, guilt gets in the way of spiritual growth.

How can you grow when you feel so bad all of the time? It feels like having a noose around your neck that's attached to an anvil-it's heavy and restrictive. There are varying degrees of guilt and they all are negative emotions, they have no place in anyone's life. This thing called *guilt* allows others to control or be controlled, which goes against the spirit who has a divine nature. Guilt is a parent emotion to manipulation, once someone places the guilt inside of your mind-they are able to easily manipulate you or the situation.

If you do something negative towards another person, then the guilt there is semi-productive. That is the time to make amends and then shut the door on the guilt, don't just stay there and make a home with it, guilt was not meant to be a life partner with you.

As we move out of guilt, we may feel a void, so we must replace it with love, kindness, respect, honor and self confidence. With love, guilt cannot penetrate our being. With kindness, guilt cannot fester because we are living in a kind and caring manner. With respect and honor, we wish to act and think in a positive and productive way, so we are keeping anything harmful away from us. Self confidence will not allow us to be controlled or to control another person, it is our shield from guilt. We begin to experience the Source of everything good that's in this world. We no longer desire to blame ourselves or anyone else for the parts of our lives that bring us pain and suffering. There is no one to blame, life is just what happens and how we choose to handle it.

The idea is for us to live our lives, doing our best and accepting the fact that sometimes our best is not good enough for us, but it is that Divine effort that we must put forward. It is when we begin to accept ourselves as human beings, flaws and perfections, do we become whole and complete individuals-free from guilt, free from shame and free to love, honor and respect ourselves and others?

TODAY THIS IS HOW I START RELEASING MYSELF FROM GUILT!

_____
_____
_____
_____
_____
_____
_____
_____
_____
_____
_____
_____
_____
_____
_____
_____
_____
_____

Pay Attention

God wants our attention, but sometimes we are too busy to realize it.
It's like God would have to call us on our cell phones, shoot us an email or send a fax
Just for us to get the intended message for that moment, situation or time.
I guess a text message would do, but then we'd have to respond immediately,
instead of a 'when I get more time' reply.
It's time to slow down or completely stop just to hear the words that are coming out of God's mouth. Time to listen and time to understand.

CHAPTER FIVE
Spiritual ADHD

Clouds

Dark Clouds cover the blue brightness-the sky begins to cry. Heavy tears fall upon the places where people walk. Those tears fall silently upon souls as they look for shelter. Tears slow down as the light reappears and dry up and away as the rainbow brings color to the sky.

Spiritual ADHD

Do you or someone you know have Spiritual ADHD? If you answer yes to any of these statements, then chances are you or someone you know does?
- When you can't or won't sit still and focus on the really important aspects of life.
- When you fail to hear the Divine words or directions that could allow you to live a fuller and richer life.
- When you will do anything so you don't listen to that inner voice talking to you.

What in your life needs more of your time and energy, more importantly, what in your life has that time and energy that it does not deserve? We can go through or lives giving all of the wrong things our focus, a dead-end job, a destructive relationship, an old car that does more draining of your bank account than it does transporting you from point A to point B. Are you giving your energy to doing nothing with your time, thinking about getting that job, thinking about losing that last ten pounds. Are you wondering how life would have been different, if you just had listened to your mother or father? The problem is not just what you are thinking; the problem is our lack of action. Don't try to do it, do it, either you do something or you don't. Most people may not have chosen their circumstances in life, but all of us get to a point where we can make changes to some things in our lives; it is up to us, whether or not we do it.

We are our own best friend; we should know ourselves better than anyone else. We should want better for ourselves than anyone else wants for us. The reality is that we seldom see ourselves as others do. We stand in front of the mirror, but do not see our true essence. We may see an average person with average abilities or see a phenomenal person whom we love and admire; it's all in our perception.

Our new focus is on ourselves-to see the real greatness in ourselves, as others who love us do and as God does. The energy we use to promote ourselves in a good light, is energy well spent. From this point on, it is our right and our duty to find that one thing that brings us happiness, fulfillment and passion and pursue it. Ask for guidance from your Divine Source and you will watch your life unfolding right before your very eyes. If you spend one hour just thinking about what you wish you could do, you have just wasted sixty precious minutes of your life. Don't just think about it, act on the direction given and know that this is your life…live it!!!

<u>WHERE IS MY FOCUS, HOW DO I GET IT TO WHERE IT SHOULD BE?</u>

CHAPTER SIX
Dark Times Light

After-all, you

After the love is gone, after the job has ended, after your love has left you, after the money is depleted, after everything is gone, you still have you.

The question is; which *you* are you willing to deal with? The scared, unfulfilled *you* or the strong, see life a challenge waiting to be met, *you*?

The choice is yours and yours alone to make. Which *you* can *you* live with?

Dark Times Light

The dark times are the times when we cannot see the ever-present light of God. The dark seemingly takes over and we lose sight of any form of daylight. The objective however, is not to become lost in the dark, but to visualize the light. You can run a thousand miles in the wrong direction and still be in the dark, however, you can take one step towards God you will be blinded by the magnificent light. Once the light surrounds you, it is hard to believe that we once allowed to dark to consume us.

See, the dark needs your permission to grab you and consume your being; otherwise you can proceed normally and grow right through life's trials and tribulations. All life is, is a series of situations, joys, pains, chance meetings and trials. They all come and go, leaving room for the next set of situations, etc.

God does not intend for His/Her people to be in the dark and certainly not live in darkness. The dark is for sleeping, but otherwise the dark in not productive mentally, physically or spiritually. "Anything that's done in the dark, comes to the light." This old proverb speaks volumes, saying how the dark can become a breeding place for negativity. Not until the dark is dissolved by light, can the negative be turned into a positive.

People live in the dark when they hide certain parts of themselves or cover up lies about themselves or their lives, there is freedom in truth. The source of what is hidden creates a great deal of stress. Many times after a person is exposed-a lie is revealed or a situation is discovered, that individual may have to deal with consequences, but there is a sense of relief in a strange sort of way. The dark oftentimes becomes equated with stress, doubt, anger and other negative emotions. The light reflects on itself, it equals relief, happiness and peace of mind.

There is nothing like living in the light. God's light is pure and filled with love and understanding. It is that light that leads us to The Other Side/Heaven at the end of this journey here.

When you find that the dark has a hold on you and you feel like you have no way of releasing it; think of yourself in the Light of God and imagine the Holy Spirit/God Center/Your Supreme Deity, taking your hand and leading you from the darkness. I would advise you to be open to the times when you do not feel the veil of darkness lifting from you after countless meditations. In some cases of depression or similar symptoms, it would be wise to seek assistance from a Mental Health Professional. God created these people to help others and there is absolutely, nothing wrong with you seeking help. We all need someone else's assistance in some form on a daily basis. This just makes you human, not crazy or flawed in any way. You are God personified, you are a creation of something great and it's alright to seek and receive help. We are all truly special in our own skin; we are here on this earth for our own special purpose. Never forget that.

As sons and daughters of God/The Creator, we are able not only to bask in Divine light, we are able to emit and transmit our light to others. Every time we smile at someone, every time we help a small child or an elderly person, we transmit our light to someone else and sending them a ray of God's light. Many times we transmit that light and do not realize it. Many of our good deeds are seen by another but we are not aware of it, this allows our light to be transmitted to them effortlessly.

Light is life and life is light, they go hand in hand. Whenever you send someone else your light, you give them more life, more reasons to smile, more reason to live. This journey called life is difficult sometimes, but as I have heard growing up: "Don't stress about life, nobody gets out alive anyway." While we are here on this earth, we give and receive light and enjoy the God given ability to make each day count, living in and loving in the Greater Divine Light of God. Go into the world giving *life* and *light*…And so it is.

TODAY I FIND MY WAY TO THE LIGHT BY…?

CHAPTER SEVEN
Build, Build and Rebuild

Divine Representation

I am a real person; I represent all nations and cultures. I dance to the drums of ancient Africa and I bathe in the Nile. I am in France; I stand as tall as the Eiffel tower in a place that appreciates my strength and for who I am.
I walk in the sands of the Caribbean, letting the breeze hit my face ever so gently.
I represent to Asian countries letting my Yin unite with my Yang, my love for Jade Buddha statues centering me. Inhaling the sweet scent of Cumin and Curry, as I dance the dance of love for all to see. I look to the east towards Mecca and bow down respect for the Arab Nations. My Native American ties bring me closer to nature and my eyes speak stories about divine animals and Great Spirits who protect us. I am in the hills of Italy, I am in the snow in Siberia, I am in the trees of the rainforests,
I am in the mountains of Tibet.
I represent all nations, all colors, all creeds, all religions, all cultures, all ages, all sexes, all lifestyles, all people for all time.
All...I represent all. We are one.

Build, Build and Rebuild

Building your life is like building a house. It begins by laying a strong foundation, sometimes our foundations are not that strong and the bricks that we put on top do not last, but the great thing is, that we can rebuild over and over again until it is right. Starting over may be exhausting work, but can be done.

Each accomplishment, each triumph, each good or bad experience, are like your bricks. Each brick is equal and works together to build your house (life). The cement that holds your life together, are your thoughts, hopes, dreams. Even your so-called negative thoughts tie into this because you are putting them into the cement. The thoughts good and bad bring about a balance to your house so that once your house settles; it will remain in balance, giving your life polarity. You cannot appreciate what is good until you know what the bad feels like. Now that you have your foundation-you have your house to build.

Building your house takes thought and energy, the right thoughts and energy can create a beautiful and strong dwelling. Once your house is built, you must select the type of roof that will sit above you. Is your roof made of slate or aluminum, are there tiles or shingles? It does not matter what the material is, the important thing is that the roof is solid and strong and will protect you from the elements. Your house is your vision of love in your life; your roof is your connection to your own Higher Power/God. Once you are open to building your new life, the old house/life is replaced with a much better one. Your relationship with God is stronger, hence the supportive rooftop. Whenever you look upward, you feel a sense of security and divine love.

Your house/life is empty, now it's time to decide who and what will go on the inside. What kind of greenery will surround the outside?

Visualize the colors that will be painted on the inside, what colors make you happy and make you feel as if you can relax in this space. Your hopes and dreams are safely cemented in, now you have to activate them with your actions. Time to decorate, now if you do not put your all into your home, at times a brick may fall out and hit you in the head just to remind you of the promise you made to yourself-to build a whole new life. That will be only a test to see how committed you are to building and maintaining your brand new home/life.

As you decide what and who belongs in your house, you must first look inside of yourself and ponder carefully on who deserves that front row seat in your life.

Think of it as you have the house of your dreams, you would not pick up an old smelly piece of furniture from the dumpster as decoration for your home. It is the same with people and situations, you must be careful about who and what is in your house with you. You have choices, you can limit the negative and accentuate the positive in your life just by the wave of your hand. If you make a mistake and allow something to enter your dwelling that is not good for you, you can fix it-you can just start 'cleaning your house', it may be exhausting work, but it also can be done. All of the negativity, hurt and pain can be tossed into yesterday's garbage and each day a new beginning emerges. Build anew and enjoy every minute of it, each teardrop, each drop of sweat and every laugh will make your house more beautiful than before.

Happy Building!! Happy Living!!

WHAT AM I BUILDING & WHAT DO I WANT TO BUILD?

Me

There is no one quite like *me*; I am unique and loveable in my present form. This is my day and I intend to use it to benefit *me* and those around *me*. There is no one better than *me*, more beautiful than *me* and I challenge anyone to try and change this knowledge that is deep inside of *me*. As I walk this journey of life, I fall deeper in love with who I am. The best person in the world is *me*, there is no one like *me* and I embrace the person who was created different than anyone else in the universe. *Me*, there is no pressure to think feel or act like anyone else. There is no jealousy of anyone else's lives, because my journey is mine alone and I will make the best out of each and every day. *Me*, I am Love personified and I know that I am that direct link to the Divine. *Me*, I am.

Ode to 'Love'

Thank you 'love' for showing me
that you are not a myth
Much gratitude to you for making me
feel so happy and so good.
Love, I am grateful for you
Not being fake, but for being real.
Love you showed me a behavior,
not words that what makes me feel.
Love, thank you for showing me that
not only you make me feel good
and you can also cause me to feel pain.
I used to live off of your sunshine
I didn't know you could also make it
rain. Love, you bring joy, happiness,
confusion and tears
Yet you are that one emotion that is
eternal. Thank you love for showing me
what to look for
So next time love comes my way,
I won't expect less, I'll accept more.

CHAPTER EIGHT
Future Shock

"Always remain true to who you are, no longer a prisoner of someone else's jail. I am free, I love freely, I live freely."

Future Shock

Our futures are as uncertain as the wind. You never know which way it will blow, you'll never know which direction you will go. You have the present and for that moment that is all you have, that is, until tomorrow comes and today's future's becomes tomorrow's present.

Now this is a very simple concept, since everyone knows that as the sun sets and rises, the days will go by in the same manner every day. What we don't always realize is, how much time we waste wondering about what will happen in the future and not preparing for what we want to have happen. We waste time looking back at something that used to be or that never really was, except in our own minds. The future, past and present are right now and we have to find away to live in it with appreciation, not apprehension.

We all have childhood memories and old home footage that we can go back and reflect on the good times, and not so good times. Remember how you felt going to a friend's house and you are subjected to, too many of the home movies or the endless flow of pictures with people that you will probably never meet. At that time, you want the earth to come up and swallow you, just so you wouldn't have to endure such boredom and torture. Well look at what you are doing to yourself, you replay the same old movies in your head, the same old pictures and the same situations over and over until your mind has had enough, until your memories aid in your own self-torture.

There is nothing wrong with nostalgia, but living in the past is a dangerous place for the otherwise productive mind. It's like driving forward, but you keep looking in the rear view mirror then BAM!! Now you've hit someone else, because you were so immersed in your old home movies.

Bring yourself to the here and now, in order to make your present self more productive and let the future will take care of itself.

Having an appreciation for what is playing right in front of your face, gives your life perspective and allows your thoughts to become clear and more focused when the future finally arrives. For some reason we are afraid of what's around the corner, but there is absolutely no need for fear because, all the future is; is the appreciation of now being manifested at a later time. All things that we do now are affecting the person that we will be in the future. So no more fear, just enjoy where you are and make it beautiful so it won't be an old movie that has to be re-played over again. Create the peaceful tomorrow by becoming spiritual and emotionally grounded today.

<u>MY GIFT FOR MYSELF IS TO LIVE IN THE PRESENT</u>
<u>(I RELEASE)</u>

_____

_____

_____

_____

_____

_____

_____

_____

_____

_____

_____

_____

_____

_____

_____

_____

_____

_____

_____

_____

CHAPTER NINE
What In The World Do You Want

Mirror Images

What you give is what you will receive into your life, your mind and your space.

When you give out animosity and hatred, it comes back to you triple-fold. When you give good vibrations, positive energy and love, it comes to you ten times as strong and you will enjoy lasting effects over and over. The mirrors of your life are the example of the way that you are living.

Give love and your love will grow stronger every day, trust others and you will become secure within yourself. This life is full of mirrors and you are the deciding factor on what you will see when you look, face to face.

What In The World Do You Want

Is there any time in your life where you can truly know what you really want out of your life, your current situation, your job, your love life or your finances? What is it that you really want? When you really look at that question, it complicates things. You have to look deep inside of yourself to not only find what you want, but why do you want it? Your motivation and your desire must match-be equally yoked, so to speak. You motive behind your behavior is the most important factor. If you are not motivated, then your actions will either be slow or non-existent, either way the desire is not being fulfilled. The Bible says, "Faith without works is dead", saying that your actions need to meet your thoughts or words, or else nothing will happen.

One of the most important motives is self improvement. Self improvement wears many hats; you may have a desire to learn something different by taking a class or gaining financial independence by owning a business. There are many types of self improvement, it doesn't have to be a great earth-shattering movement, sometimes, and it's the accomplishing of smaller goals that create the greatest impact. The reason behind the action can be as important as or more important than the action itself. The first question should be: "Why do I want to do that thing or become this type of person?" The answers may surprise you. Once you ask the question, you must begin preparing for the answer.

The single most important thing in finding out what you want in any situation or time, is to be completely honest with yourself. What does your mind say to your heart? What is your heart's reply to the mind's questions? There has to be that internal integrity going on in order to move forward in any way. Being true to yourself is also a form of self love. You must be honest with *yourself*, love *yourself* and develop the motivation from within *yourself* to fit the desires that you have lined up for *yourself*.

Go and chase that desire, if it is for you, the chase will not seem so challenging, in fact, the challenge will be a welcome one, because you will have already felt the warmth of the light at the end of the tunnel. There is nothing greater than a sense of accomplishment, because it shows you your greatness, it shows your level of faith and more importantly, it shows you that God is working in your favor as long as you trust and believe that you are not alone in your struggle.

WHAT IN THE WORLD DO I WANT?

CHAPTER TEN
Life's What If's

The sun shines in places where only darkens used to dwell. Salt and pepper images have evolved into a rainbow of possibilities. Opened are the once closed eyes and smiling are the lips that would not move. Eyes glisten where tears used to flow and as the day comes in and the sun rises, the breeze says: "All is well."

Life's What If's

There is nothing funnier than looking at life's what ifs after the fact and that thing that you worried, about simply did not exist. Some of us spend so much time, wasted time, wondering 'what if', and the 'what if' is always something bad or negative. When you look at your life, you are so focused on what could happen, that you may not have seen the reality of what has actually transpired. One way to break a bad habit, is to work on it one day at a time. Instead of wondering what if I get fired, get hit by a train, or go way out in left field-what if I die? Well if you die, you won't be wondering 'what if' anymore, but if you are alive-you are allowing fear to overtake your life. What if, you end up happier than you have ever been? What if you find that long lost item that had so much sentimental value? What if you end up with more money than you can spend in one lifetime or more love than you can handle in one lifetime? In one lifetime, you can accomplish more than you ever thought possible, it's all in how you look at your life and what you want from it. Begin by looking at your life in a positive way-seeing the good things, not bad. You focus on the good memories of your past, not the traumatic events. Once you begin to see you and your life in the best possible light, you can begin to unfold all of the petals of the flower called 'you'.

"Here's to being the best you, that you can be."

***BONUS QUESTION: YEAH, WHAT IF?**

_____

_____

_____

_____

_____

_____

THE PURCHASE

I went to the store today and purchased a brand new me.
I came with a compassionate heart, and a soul that made even gold seem dull.
I came with pearly white teeth so shiny that even in the brightest of days, my smile could lighten any place I'm in.
I asked for love to flow through me endlessly, and that I would never run out of it.
I requested a tongue made of Sweetgrass, so that only words of kindness would be spoken, because there are already too many other words being spoken.
I received a transparent soul, that way others will know exactly who I am;
I'd never have to pretend to be anything other than my wonderful, beautiful self.
I came with the ability to see the good in anyone and anything, seeing God's grace in all creation.
I came with more beauty than I'd ever be able to describe, I am beauty personified and I am truly a gift to myself, from myself.
I went to the store today and received a brand new me.

CHAPTER ELEVEN
A Look At Relationships or Are Relationships Looking at Us?

Loving Me

Gentle caresses, words of praise, adoring looks and happy feelings.
Late night talks, daytime silence, inner voices keeping loneliness away.
A soul resting, spiritual peace...
As the day turns to night again, I look in the mirror and say...
"You're wonderful, beautiful and I love you very much."

<u>A Look At Relationships or Are Relationships Looking at Us?</u>

As we grow older and hopefully wiser, we are constantly learning about having various types of relationships. These are the things that create our outlooks on life and our feelings towards ourselves and others. In our earliest years, our minds and spirits were shaped by those who took care of us, our first intimate relationships. We were loved, held, fed and talked to in voices that made us smile-if we were blessed to have that type of family. Some of us may have had different, not so warm and fuzzy childhood experiences, but nonetheless, we are here learning about ourselves and those around us.

What are we to gain by having relationships? The largest gain is the lessons that we learn about ourselves, yes, we are to experience love but there are many life lessons that are attached to relationships. Believe it or not a relationship teaches us more about ourselves than it does about the other person. We choose to either be in a loving and nurturing relationship or we choose someone or a circumstance that is detrimental to our lives and our spiritual and emotional growth. You can tell the level of self esteem a person possesses by the people that he or she choses as life associates or friends. Those in abusive, destructive or unproductive relationships with a significant other, are actually showing the outward product of an inward thought or feeling. If you feel good about yourself and truly love 'the skin you're in', then no one can make you feel otherwise-you will not attract anyone who feels any differently towards you or themselves.

People can misrepresent themselves as the person that you may be looking for, however, it takes that 'real' self love to be willing and able to see a person for who and what they really are.

More times than not people are forced or choose to settle for conditions that are beneath them spiritually, not saying that someone is better or worse than us, but the situation itself does more harm than good. Situations are not a direct representation of the singular person in the relationship; it is the representation of the collaboration of the two people involved. It's like the old saying "There's someone for everyone." There is a person that cultivates the inner you and if you are not with that person, you will not feel as if you are in the right place. It can be very painful for you and the people that care for you.

The most important key to having, maintaining and being happy in any type of relationship, is honoring yourself completely. When you are honoring yourself in the truest sense of the word, there are certain situations and people that cannot be allowed into your personal space without your permission. When you honor yourself, you see what is really there and not what you'd like to see there. Your mind will not allow you to fool it with fantasy and ego trips. Truly honoring what you feel makes you see the things that may otherwise go unnoticed. When you honor yourself, you are also loving, cherishing and obeying yourself. It becomes a marriage of sorts, because you are making a commitment to a better you and not letting anything divide and conquer your pact with yourself.

In many of our daily relationships, we miss the subtle things that come our way that do not honor us, for instance, people dangle carrots in front of us or we dangle from a string hoping for that better day to come and sometimes it never does. This is a prime example of not being honored.

Let's use the following scenario:
If you are on the edge of a cliff, most of your body is suspended in mid-air, would you rather have someone throw you a string or a rope? Well depending on what arrived first, some may grab onto the string, the string came first-it resembled a rope-it's almost as good as a rope, right? WRONG! The string is thin, it will not last very

long, the string has a tendency to cut if held onto for too long and the holder of the string knows this, but will throw it to you anyway just to test you. Now if you wait for the rope, the rope is strong, long-lasting and has the capability to hold you for a longer period of time, therefore giving you ability to save yourself or give yourself the honor and commitment that you need, so to speak. If you think about your daily business or personal relationships, has someone ever held you by a string?

The string is the sign of false promises or the feeling that something is, when it isn't.

The rope is a sign of strength, hope and possibility. Honor yourself-take the rope and never let anyone entice you with a piece of thread.

WHAT ARE MY RELATIONSHIPS SAYING ABOUT ME?

CHAPTER TWELVE
Respect, Nothing More-Nothing Less

"If you know yourself better than anyone else and you do, it should be easy to love and cherish the divine and eternal creation that you are."

Respect, Nothing More-Nothing Less

When you think of respect and what it means to you and those around you. Most people would rather have respect than love. Respect is a thought and a behavior, when you think a certain way, you will act accordingly. There are me any families or other relationships that seem to have some type of love and a lack of respect, the real idea of love does not really exist because of the behaviors shown towards one to another. When you have a healthy respect for an individual or yourself, you display certain good behaviors that exhibit your feelings and the same goes when you lack respect or self respect-you create negative actions or think negative thoughts. Respect is such an important issue in our daily lives, that there are songs and cliques about it. Aretha spelled it out and even an old comedian once complained of not being able to get any respect. We are the physical and human representation of

God. When we respect one another we are, in essence, respecting God. On the flip side, to disrespect one another is to disrespect God. It is important to gain a strong and healthy respect for yourself. When you are a self-respecting individual, there are certain behaviors or actions you will not display.

For example, a female child or teenage girl bullies others, dresses or acts older than her years or acts out in a sexual way, shows lack of self-respect-there may be a reason, but it's a lack of self respect nonetheless. A teen boy who acts aggressively towards others, treats others in an unkind manner or uses himself in a sexually inappropriate way, shows lack of self-respect, what is the reason? If the teenagers act appropriately towards those of the opposite and same sexes, treat authority figures as such, there is a level of self-respect there, it's not necessarily love but they are showing a degree of respect. The same goes for the opposite actions, when you treat others well, it is a manifestation of how you feel about yourself. Each person's level of self-respect is different from someone else's; it's an individual feeling or action. What works for one person, may not work for another-except each one of us having the utmost respect for God, for life, for people and animals, for nature and yourself that you can give. If the way a person speaks to you or treats you, makes you feel disrespected, honor those feelings and make them known. If that person refuses to change, you can respect yourself and walk away from that person for good. The true test of a person's respect level is if they continue those actions repeatedly, now you have the right to demand respect. "Respect is earned!" we have been told throughout our lives, but how is it earned? As human beings, we earn it by our Divine birthright; it is our behavior that dictates the level and the kind of respect that we earn. Let's make a conscious choice to respect one another as it was intended to be, let us collectively show love through respect and watch the world grow into a better place.

<u>WHAT DOES RESPECT MEAN TO ME AND DO I HAVE IT IN MY LIFE?</u>

CHAPTER THIRTEEN
Life's Miracles

The sand, the trees, the water and the sky: All God's Miracles

<u>Miracles</u>

**Right before my eyes, several miracles happened at one time.
The sun came up, flowers started to bloom,
a cat had its morning stretch and I danced, a dance of freedom.**

**Right in front of me, behind me a and all around me.
Several miracles happened,
more than my eyes could see.
The clouds rained, then dried to a nice fluffy white. The waves of the ocean played touch and go with the shore and I...I played alone in the sand, absorbing all of the miracles taking place.**

**In a span of little hours, millions of miracles occurred.
Babies were welcomed into the world.
Grass grew so the children could walk barefoot on top of it. Music still played softly in the background
While miracles too place, too many to mention...Millions**

LIFE'S MIRACLES

In the middle of all of our comings and goings, we don't always stop and value those seemingly small miracles in our lives. The miracles of good health, safety, peaceful surroundings, life coming into the world and just waking up to do it all over again in a new day is a miracle. Oftentimes miracles are overlooked until something tragic happens, then we see the true miracles, that we have taken for granted.

Because we wake up to the sun blazing into our faces, we take that for granted. Just because we have full lives and many things to do, we feel that our life here is too busy to end "I have to do this or I have to have that", never taking the time to look at all that life has to offer. Life is good because we are here for a reason, a purpose and it is our job to figure out what our purpose is and how to go about fulfilling it. Think of it this way, if you were told that you had 24 hours to live, even 48, let's even give you one week left here before you graduated to the Spirit World, what would be your actions, your reactions, your thoughts? Whom would you visit? Where would you go? What things would you try that were once dreams deferred? Think hard because you don't have extra time to waste and squander away-you must take action now.

Since our time here is short, it is also just as important to live as though each day is our last one on this earth. Don't withhold love, good deeds and forgiveness. Don't wait for the so-called right time to do great things, now is the right time, so let's make the best out of this time in the now. The true miracle happens each time we wake up and the sun is blazing into our eyes and we get a chance to make something new happen in our lives and the lives of those whom we touch.

YOU ARE A MIRACLE! SAY IT!!!

"I AM A MIRACLE, I AM A MIRACLE, I AM A MIRACLE!"

LIFE AND MORE

I love life and all that is in it. I enjoy the good times and I learn from the bad.
Lessons learned, some easier than others, knowledge gained finally.
I live life and grab onto every chance for all that it has to give to me.
Thoughts giving birth to things; ideas bringing forth many creations.
I respect life and all that it represents. Life is one thing that cannot be replaced.
Learning and giving, understanding that life is beautiful, every second, every breath, everyone for everyday.

CHAPTER FOURTEEN
Taking Back What's Yours

"Loving yourself is an ongoing process, it must be worked on and practiced day by day, hour by hour and in some cases-second by second. Self love is not an over inflated ego or not loving those around you. Self love is the polar opposite and radiates light everywhere it touches."

Taking Back What's Yours

As human beings, we are subject and even expected to make major mistakes in our lives. The great part about that; is the recovery process. In every situation, whether it be a physical or mental issue, recovery is the key in moving forward. When watching a football game and a team member fumbles the ball, the best way for the team to redeem themselves is to recover the ball. In life's game, we should honor our ability to recover whatever it is that we feel that we've lost. One of the most important things to recover in life is you. We tend to give away major parts of ourselves to the wrong people, the most stressful jobs, bad decisions and other self defeating situations; however, we have the power to get it all back in a blink of an eye. The first and most important step is to first decide that you want your power back, and then take the first step. Each step does not have to be a major one, but a step nonetheless. We may fall or step backwards in this unchartered zone, but again, recovery is the key to moving forward.

In any situation where change is required, there are many recoveries being made, remember, you are making a change in your life and with change, there are obstacles and mistakes, but you don't stop-you keep moving on. Don't take the time to beat yourself up during this time, feeding negative feelings and energy is unproductive at now, in fact it's unproductive at all times. Starve the negative and feed what's positive, celebrate each small victory as a step in getting back what is yours.

There is no loss when you are taking your power back, it may 'feel' like a loss, but the rewards that you sow once you have completed this part of your journey, reap huge gains, so big in fact, you will wonder what took you so long to get started.

The power to live a fulfilling life is in your hands, as humans, we can erase some mistakes and learn to live with others, either way you should always remember what is yours and that you have complete authority over it. You have the power to dictate what situations belong in your life, as long as you can breathe, you can make a change.

I RECLAIM!!!!!

CHAPTER FIFTEEN

From Caterpillars to Butterflies

I AFFIRM...

I affirm that I will love complete and without condition.

I affirm that if it feels bad or harmful to me, I will let it go without regret.

I affirm that I will wake up with an attitude of gratitude on my mind and lips.

I affirm that God will lead my steps and pick me up when I stumble on my own.

I affirm that all is good and all is God.

I affirm that the unpleasant situations are lessons for me to learn from or to teach others.

I affirm that my life will not be in vain, I will live each day to the fullest.

And I also affirm that I will give just as I have been given...completely.

FROM CATERPILLARS TO BUTTERFLIES

The times in life where you are eating dirt and living as if each day is 48 hours long. that is when your view of the situation can change the situation itself. Life may seem like it's not going to get any better and that's when the blessing will unexpectedly will fall right into your lap. Take a lesson from out fellow creature on this earth, the caterpillar, it does not fly, it just moves around on the ground. It is seen as a slimy little being and no one wants to touch it or even look at it. At an appointed time, the caterpillar listens to its *God-voice* inside and prepares to live inside the cocoon. He has never lived in this cocoon but listening to nature, he goes and prepares it for his slumber. Once he has slept or whatever they do in there, he/she emerges beautiful and able to fly from one place to another. The first step is being born, secondly going with nature and not against it, thirdly being still to see what is to come next and lastly growing into a more peaceful and beautiful person. If we are to engage in our own journey, we must follow the example of the butterfly. Once we are still and listening to the inner voice, we will emerge with more wisdom, understanding and ability to cope with whatever comes into our lives. Our own private metamorphosis is amazing.

The secret to enjoying the life of a butterfly is to learn to conquer the thinking of a caterpillar, you cannot move forward with backward thinking-it is like trying to move, but each one of your legs wish to go in two separate directions-it is not possible-you are stagnated and left frustrated and exhausted from the unproductive action.

"As I crawl on the ground, getting dirt in my mouth, I can see the big picture- that one day I will soar amongst the clouds and sing along with the birds."

MY METAMORPHOSIS IS?

CHAPTER SIXTEEN
The Power to Create or Destroy

"As the Phoenix and the Lotus rise and bloom so do I. Never let adversity stop you, it's just there to strengthen your legs, so you can climb over it."

THE POWER TO CREATE OR DESTROY

Anyone who has children or has some type of relationship with one or more children has tremendous power in their hands. There is a power to either create greatness or destroy what could have been great. Words of encouragement go a long way; however words of negativity go even further, they can cause an individual to spiral into a world of nothingness. When one has the power to give life (not just in the physical sense), but in the spiritual sense, it is vital that what is projected is built on the principles of love. Oh you can love someone and unconsciously destroy that person, what you feel about yourself can reflect in ways that you may not understand. You can use fear, jealousy, revenge or even ignorance as a tool to destroy what could potentially be a great person who could have done great things or you can turn it around completely and create greatness.

Obstacles are not the problem, lack of support in how we overcome them is.

Watch your words around innocent ears, they absorb more of our thoughts and feelings than we could ever imagine. Children learn all behaviors and most emulate what they see. To tell a child that their dreams and aspirations are impossible is like throwing water on a fire meant to keep you warm. Using fear to keep someone from trying something new creates a spirit of fear and uncertainly throughout that person's lifetime. It also blocks potential blessings from the one who instills fear and the one that absorbs it.

Children look at the role models in their young lives and all during the growth process for direction, there is always one person that sticks out in that child's mind as the one who had the greatest affect on them as individuals.

Some teachers are acknowledged for the understanding or compassion that was given to a child that he or she was lacking at home or anywhere else. Sometimes it's a coach, shopkeeper or the old man/woman who lived at the end of the block, role models come in all shapes, sizes, ages and colors.

It is equally important to become that child and give words of love and encouragement to ourselves. We are in a position of power in our lives, the power to destroy or the power to create something great, that greatness that lies deep within our psyche. I have observed that people are more comfortable speaking of their flaws than they are about the good things that represent them.

A woman will complain about her weight, skin or some other part of herself and that is usual, but what if that same woman told others, how great she thought she was, or how she felt that she was at her perfect weight and marveled at the beauty of her own complexion. Since some of us are not comfortable with ourselves, we may view this woman as conceited or arrogant, when all she is really doing is recognizing and bringing forth her God-given greatness.

It is important to take each day, from now on and stand in the mirror and tell yourself either aloud or in your mind (your choice) how great you are. State the things that you like about yourself, they don't need to be physical attributes, it can be anything that you find that makes you feel good about being you. Do not take those things for granted, they are what is unique and wonderful about the person that you are.

Try it, do it and create greatness within yourself and those around you.

---Namaste

(The Divine in me salutes the Divine in You)

THE GREATNESS THAT I CREATE COMES FROM…?

THE COLOR BLUE

Sometimes I look at the color blue
it doesn't make me sad like the songs
imply.
It actually makes me think of life and
beauty, like the water, and the day
and night sky.
The many shades are as vast as the
earth itself.
With its royals and assures, navies
and electrics, each one representing
one feeling or another.
Some feelings are calm and classic
while others wild and eclectic.
Sometimes I look at the color blue
and it warms my heart from the
inside out like chakras illuminating
from our bodies, the color blue is one
I cannot live without.

CHAPTER SEVENTEEN

"Love comes in the most unlikely places. Sometimes you are hit with a revelation and you are never the same. Keep love in your hearts and enjoy life to the fullest."

SOMETIMES EXPECTATIONS ARE DISAPPOINTMENTS IN DISGUISE

We all do it, we place some sort of value on a person, or a thing and expect a certain result. Sometimes those results do not look that way that we anticipated and that is when our disappointment and negative feelings start to surface. Being that we are all human, there are no superheroes wandering the face of the earth, we need to realize that fact. We have to examine the what, why and how of our expectations and with whom we are putting our feelings into to give that person the power to change our thoughts or not live up to 'our' expectations.

Love is a huge expectation. Many do *things* in order to receive love in return, that is one of the biggest misconceptions ever. Real love is not a result of…real love just is what it is, not based on who did what or why something occurred. When you meet someone of the opposite sex with an expectation of something more happening, you run the risk of setting yourself up for a huge disappointment. The other person does not have the power to disappoint you at that point, but you are giving your power away. Male and Female relationships have been the topic of many studies for decades, yet no one has found the answers to what creates long lasting and great unions. The main issue, as it was told to me by a very wise woman, "that women and men love differently". Women love with their hearts on their sleeves, while men tend to be a bit more guarded-then women go into panic mode: "Does he or doesn't he like me?" and the man is keeping his distance, seeing if the woman is who she said she is. That creates actions that may be out of character for the woman and a feeling of insecurity for the man. The goal for many people, not all people, but many is to be loved by their significant other, but with all good things, comes bumps and bruises. You will experience highs and lows even when the right one comes along. Remember men, treat a woman the way you would want your daughter, sister or mother treated by a man, no lies, games and distance, be honest. Women, treat the man like you would want your son, brother or father treated. No lies, games and attitude problems. We all want respect, honor and love, but we also have to learn to give it just as well.

I would say that in order to expect something, the first order of business is to actually know what that something really is and what it looks like. We ask for things and once we receive them, they do not look or feel the way that we anticipated, classic example of expectation=disappointment.

I have been guilty of this type of thinking many times. When you do a job well for an employer, you may *expect* to be rewarded with raises or a promotion, but in reality, you may not even get that pat on the back that you were counting on.

Now how does that affect you? How does that affect your future performance on that same job when you are asked to do something extra? More importantly, was there ever a thought of doing something for the sake of doing it and any reward that came with it, would be an extra added bonus? This would have helped tremendously because you will not be feeling disappointed.

How many women have lived with or dated men with the expectation that marriage would happen within a certain timeline or even at all?

How many parents pushed their children into careers or schooling that would be financially beneficial in the future, only to have that child say "I want to follow my heart or campaign for world peace". Now world peace is a beautiful thing, it may not pay much, but that child is happy. The parent expected the child to create a different reality, now an expectation attached to disappointment has shown up.

As we venture into our future, we need to realign ourselves with the spiritual side of expectation. There are things that we expect that can create beauty in our lives, we expect the sun to come out every morning and the stars to come out at night, and on those times where it is too cloudy to see both, we can rest in the knowledge that even though we can't see it, the stars and the sun are still there waiting for us and for us. With that being said, we know that our expectations were met, just in a different fashion. Learn to look at the origin of your expectations, so that there are more successes than there are failures. See them as learning experiences and not negative moments, there is little disappointment in that. Without effective communication with oneself, expectations are unknown and therefore become disappointments for sure.

<u>AS I VENTURE FORWARD, MY EXPECTATIONS ARE…?</u>

_____

_____

_____

_____

_____

_____

_____

_____

_____

_____

_____

_____

_____

_____

_____

_____

_____

_____

_____

_____

_____

CHAPTER EIGHTEEN
God's Hand

"Remembering who we really are is the first step in awakening to our spiritual path. Throughout the journey from birth to death, many people choose to question life, strive for improvement, seek out knowledge, and search for the divine. Simply put, this is the essence of spirituality."

GOD'S HAND

When something is too much for you to handle, it is important to realize that our limitations exist for a reason. Many times we bite off more than we can chew, but in the end, we have to face the reality that: "This is a job for 'Divine Intervention', not Superman."

We tend to worry about the outcome of a situation because our limited thinking and abilities make us insecure about letting go and not having control. In order to have the 'best' result, we need to move aside and let God handle the situation. The biggest lesson in this life is to learn that the very second we take our hands off of a person, situation or a thing, God's hand immediately takes over. Many times we handle a situation and actually have no idea of the current state, let alone the possible outcome. We tend to go into panic mode but soon realize that prayer and meditation mode is best.

As a parent of adult children, many would agree with me that once the child grows into adulthood, many of the values or ideals that we may have instilled in him/her may not be displayed in their behavior. Once we decide to relinquish control to the still, invisible force that controls everything around us, we can save ourselves a lot of headache or heartache. We teach them; then they decide which path works for them. As parents, mentors or other authority figures, our jobs are to guide and pray for them, but in those cases where guidance becomes control, situations arise that are not for the best. It's safe to say that most situations are best resolved by 'Divine Intervention', letting God show 'us' the correct outcome. Many of us have created disasters when we work towards the result that *we* think should be. We bump our heads a few times until the lesson is learned. As we venture into our lessons in life, we can work on our 'let go and let God' abilities. Repeat the following over and over:

"I release it, I give it to the Power greater than myself. I give what I cannot control to my Source. I relinquish control of my life.
I agree to submit my will to that of the Invisible Force."

21 THINGS I RELEASE & GIVE TO GOD

1. _____
2. _____
3. _____
4. _____
5. _____
6. _____
7. _____
8. _____
9. _____
10. _____
11. _____
12. _____
13. _____
14. _____
15. _____
16. _____
17. _____
18. _____
19. _____
20. _____
21. _____

(YOU DON'T HAVE TO STOP AT 21, KEEP IT GOING FOR THE REST OF YOUR LIFE, THOSE THINGS THAT ARE TOO BIG FOR YOU, MAKE IT A CONSISTENT HABIT OF GIVING THEM TO YOUR GOD, YOUR DIVINE ENERGY AND '_SOURCE_')

Every day, think of something new or something that needs Divine attention, then take a moment to send it upward until it is completely out of your hands.

Visualize it rising up like a helium filled balloon into the clouds-no longer within your reach into God's hands.

EVERYDAY I GROW

Every day I learn something new about life and about myself. Each day above ground is a learning experience that many times may not benefit you directly, but will allow you to help another person who is on your same path. Today is the gift that we are given in order to make tomorrow better. As we venture into the next hour, or the next day, we can rest assured that nothing in life happens in vain and it is a part of our Divine plan to learn for ourselves and to teach those who are around us or will come to us in the future. Today is our right now, we can prepare for better and more rewarding times in our immediate or distant future. Every day, we grow to become better.

(The end)

...and the beginning of something new)

Food for thought from the author…

"Don't get mad, be strong. Mad is not productive strength creates action."

"If you can't beat them, excel them. You are the only one limiting yourself"

"God made you, so if anyone has any complaints refer them to your maker."

"Life is how you see it, what you make it and where you take it."

"Strive to be better and you will be the best. Decide for yourself, not to be like the rest."

Say: "I am Great, I am good and I will live my life, just as I should, in Divine Greatness."

"A life without lessons, is not a life at all."

And last but not least:

"Don't fear what comes tomorrow, our Creator is already there waiting for us."

MORE FROM THE AUTHOR:

I hope you enjoyed reading Inspire U. If you wish to offer feedback or just want to send a friendly note to me, feel absolutely free to do so at mayskypublishing@gmail.com. I will answer your email in a timely fashion and look forward to our next venture together.

Sending you love and blessings...

"PEACE, BLESSINGS & JOY"

For additonal copies of this book please re-order online at www.createspace.com/3841880 or www.mayskypublishing.com

ABOUT THE AUTHOR

Dr. Salima N'Dulu began her spiritual studies in various traditional churches. The Episcopal Church was her first introduction to religion. During Dr. N'Dulu's life as an Episcopalian, she also attended Catholic School. This was the beginning of her open minded approach to religion in general.

Upon learning that there were other people that believed in God differently gave her a desire to learn more about various religions and spiritual outlooks. Once she experienced a variety of religions, she decided to eventually become formally educated in Religious Studies and Pastoral Counseling.

Dr. N'Dulu currently counsels and speaks to women's groups about self esteem, empowerment and spirituality.

www.ingramcontent.com/pod-product-compliance
Lightning Source LLC
Chambersburg PA
CBHW060332050426
42449CB00011B/2733